PATRONAGE

by
Mark Nicholls

This first edition published in Australia in 2019 by:

Prahran Publishing
P.O. Box 2041, Prahran, Victoria, 3181

© Copyright Mark Nicholls 2019

Mark Nicholls has asserted his legal and moral right under the Copyright Act 1968 to be identified as the author of this work.

Published by arrangement with
Prahran Publishing, Australia.

All rights are strictly reserved.

No part of this publication may be reproduced, stored in a retrieval system or transmitted, in any form or by any other means, without the publisher's prior permission in writing. Copying of this script for performance reasons is also strictly prohibited by law, either in whole or excerpts from.

This book is sold subject to the condition that it shall not, by way of trade or otherwise, be lent, resold, hired out or otherwise circulated without the publisher's prior consent in any form of binding or cover other than that in which it is published and without similar condition, including this condition, being imposed on the subsequent purchaser.

Every reasonable effort has been made to trace copyright holders of material reproduced in this book, but if any have been inadvertently overlooked the publishers would be glad to hear from them. The story, all names, characters, and incidents portrayed in this book are fictitious. No identification with actual persons past or present, places, buildings, and products is intended or should be inferred.

ISBN 978-1-922263-16-2 Paperback
ISBN 978-1-922263-17-9 eBook

Dewey: 822.4

A catalogue record for this book is available from the National Library of Australia

Performance Licensing and Royalty Payments

Mark Nicholls retains control of both the amateur and professional stage performance rights of this play. No unauthorised performance should occur without the express and written permission of the playwright.

Restriction of Alteration

There shall be no modifications of any kind to the play including deletion of dialogue (including objectionable language), changes to characters gender or names, title of the play or music without the express and written permission from the author.

Sound and Video Recordings

This play may contain stage directions to include the use of music, video or other sound recordings either in part or in whole. The author and the publisher have not sought the right to use such content and performance rights permission should be obtained separately. Permission to record audio and video recordings of all performances must also be explicitly given by the author in writing.

Author Credit

Performance rights approval requires credit be given to Mark Nicholls as the sole and exclusive author of the play. This obligation applies to the title page of every program or other advertising material distributed in connection to this play. The author's credit should appear immediately under the title of the play on all published material, and alongside no other individual. Font size of credit cannot be less than 50% of the largest letter used in the play's title.

Please email info@prahran.press
for all performance enquiries.

Dedication

for Caerwen Martin & Luke Van Ryn

About the Playwright

MARK NICHOLLS has been performing on various Melbourne stages since the age of six and has an extensive list of credits as a playwright, composer, singer, actor, producer and director. He is Senior Lecturer in Cinema Studies at the University of Melbourne where he has taught film since 1993.

He is the author of *Lost Objects of Desire: The Performances of Jeremy Irons* (2012), *Scorsese's Men: Melancholia and the Mob* (2004) and recently published articles on Italian Cinema, Powell and Pressburger's *The Red Shoes* and Sergei Diaghilev's celebrated company, The Ballets Russes.

Mark is a film critic and worked for many years on ABC Radio and for *The Age* newspaper, for which he wrote a weekly column between 2007 and 2009.

He lives in Melbourne with his partner, Ali Wirtz, and their two sons Oscar and Carlo.

Series Preface

I wrote these plays for only one reason, to perform them. I publish them here, therefore, somewhat reluctantly. They were never written to be read on the page by anyone but a treasured posy of performers that I trust to help me rescue them from it. They were certainly never conceived of as works of anything so respectable as literature. Nevertheless, I have found two reasons to overcome my reluctance and my usual roguish prejudice against readers and writers in favour of performers and punters. One reason is that putting these plays into print provides the opportunity for the most engaged of those who saw and heard them to revive and revise the experience. The other reason is archival. I wish to leave a permanent, if inadequate, record of the facts of their production over a decade, in a private space in Melbourne, for the benefit of both a small, dedicated paying audience, and for a smaller band of compulsive show-folk.

Writing these plays for the talented actors, musicians and backstage characters whose creations are recorded here, and having the privilege of working with these artists to produce them, has been the most satisfying occupation of my otherwise horrendously charmed and fascinating life.

Now that they have had their blessed release in print, these plays are beyond the concern of any motivation I had to write them. Read them, o curious one, and work it out for yourself! One motivation I will record, however, rests in the inspiration generously given by those who worked on and attended these cosy performances, and so brought their privileged, fleeting moments of theatre securely into being.

About the Play

In the age of art gallery winter blockbusters and *Carmen* on Sydney Harbour and when you can take your 'epic' pour glass of wine with you into the cinema and even fall asleep there in business class standard seating, we might wonder what remains of the artwork that is supposed to be the purpose of it all. I was thinking about this one day when I was supposed to be listening to the recording of Pablo Casals playing Bach's *Six Cello Suites* on my prematurely retro iPod 'classic'. Lulled into reflection after about four minutes, rather than concentrating on the music, I began wondering what sort of reception Pablo would get if we plonked him and his cello down in some inner Melbourne fringe venue, asked people to leave their drinks at the bar, sit on sticky ex-church hall chairs and listen to these perfect, faultlessly performed works, not for $197.50 (plus booking fee) but for the frankly insulting price a gold-coin donation. How long into the well advertised two hours and ten minutes run time (no intermission) would it take for us to reach for our phones, lose ourselves in problems at work or start plotting plausible health-related excuses to justify completely upsetting proceedings by getting up, stumbling over everyone else in row E and seeking asylum on the other side of the exit?

Exactly how much additional external stimulation do we need at a performance or exhibition before we can really settle, enjoy ourselves and appreciate it? What sort of astronomical ticket price must we pay in order to compel us to stay there and gush and bear it, when we might otherwise be far better employed on a tram flicking through Facebook? In short, if Pablo Casals ever comes to Brunswick Street, do we have the capacity to recognise him? Do we have the time?

In this play Holly clearly shares some of these concerns and is determined to make us recognise art for what it is and to force us to spend time on it. I am not sure that the rest of her gang really get it. James, Joy and Matthew are far too distracted by a sort of Luis Buñuel style group sex inclination to really have much time to respond to the simplest pleasures of art when they see or hear them. Like most of us, they are far too practical to give themselves wholeheartedly to the sort of abject madness Holly advocates. At her urging they do almost get there in the end. The sort of patronage they provide may seem somewhat degrading to their own local version of Pablo Casals, incarnated here by Rachael. But at least the solution they stumble upon is the result of a strategy that looks vaguely like something resembling the artist's own making.

CHARACTERS

HOLLY: a fifty-year-old patron of the arts.

JOY: a twenty-five-year-old medical registrar with practical ideas.

JAMES: a fifty-year-old psychiatrist and art supporter.

MATTHEW: a twenty-eight-year-old high school music teacher with some ambition.

RACHAEL: a fortyish cellist of some repute.

Patronage was first performed at Rear 4, Clifton Hill, Victoria on the 19th of June 2014 with the following cast:

Holly: Madeleine Swain

Joy: Grace Taylor

James: Mark Nicholls

Matthew: Luke Van Ryn

Rachael: Caerwen Martin

Director:	Mark Nicholls
Lighting Designer:	Oscar Wirtz
Sound Designer :	Carlo Nicholls
Rehearsal Prompter:	Gwendolen Swain
Co Producer:	Alison Wirtz

ACT ONE

The play is set now, in late summer, in the lounge room of a house in North Fitzroy. JOY enters carrying a vase of flowers and places them on a side table. Killing time, she straightens the magazines and papers on a coffee table and fusses over the room generally. When there is nothing to do, she sits down and opens a magazine and flicks though it half-heartedly. Finally, HOLLY enters [carrying a cello case] and they embrace warmly.

HOLLY: Phew! Hello darling!

JOY: You have been ages! *[She kisses her]* How long did it take you to get through Customs?

HOLLY: *[Putting the cello down]* It wasn't Customs that was the problem. It was getting a cab.

JOY: You should have let me pick you up. I wouldn't have minded. *[Looking at the cello]* So what on Earth is this? Did you buy it in London? You are not going though one of those mad instrument-learning phases again, are you?

HOLLY: It's not mine. It belongs to someone I met.

JOY: Well, what is it doing here? No wonder you got stuck in Customs. Is there anything explosive in it? Did you pack it yourself? There could be anything inside this.

HOLLY:	It's coming to stay for a while. And I didn't bring it back, Rachael did.
JOY:	And who is Rachael?
HOLLY:	I spoke to you on the phone about her. She was with me when you called the other day.
JOY:	When you were leaving?
HOLLY:	Yes. I met her in the lounge at Heathrow and we sat together all the way home.
JOY:	So why have you got her cello?
HOLLY:	She asked me to bring it in here.
JOY:	Why?
HOLLY:	Because she has gone up to bed, she's exhausted.
JOY:	What is going on? Have you asked her to stay?
HOLLY:	Yes I have. She's lovely. You will really like her.
JOY:	So, you met her on the plane and simply asked her to stay.
HOLLY:	No. There's nothing odd about it. I didn't just meet her on the plane. We sat together and talked the whole way home. She's really interesting. I get the impression she's an outstanding cellist.
JOY:	So, on the basis of a few hours in the plane together you are turning over the spare room to her and she has agreed to come and live here?

Act I 3

HOLLY: Not the spare room, darling, your old room. And it wasn't just a few hours on the plane. You know what it's like on that trip. It's so long and one hour in the air is like a week on the ground. People don't really understand that you know. That's why they make such a fuss about all that 'mile high club' business. Heavens, you talk to someone for half an hour in the plane and it's like you've met, had three intimate dinners and been on a fourteen-day walking tour together in the Cinque-Terre. No wonder people are always popping into the loo for sex.

JOY: So that's what it was?

HOLLY: Don't be ridiculous. We just got along extremely well. She happened to mention that she hadn't sorted out anywhere to live yet and so, rather than letting her go to a hotel, I asked her to come and stay for a while until she does.

JOY: So, what is she doing here? Is she moving here for good? Has she got a job?

HOLLY: You sound like the women in Customs! I gather she's coming back to do some auditions.

JOY: Coming back? Is she from here?

HOLLY: She was born here. I think she's been living in London for a while.

JOY: Hasn't she got any family to go to?

HOLLY: *[Becoming irritated]* I don't know. Actually, I didn't ask.

JOY: I bet you didn't tell James either!

HOLLY: Well, aren't you just an extraordinary little sleuth!

JOY: Well, I'm not as cute as you – picking up young girls on planes and bringing them home without even telling you husband.

HOLLY: She's not a young girl, she's at least forty, and James will certainly have no objections to this one being in the house for a while.

JOY: Oh, so she's a hottie is she?

HOLLY: *[Picking up her phone and dialling]* She's interesting and intelligent and mysterious and she doesn't put it all out there like you girls, so I don't expect you to understand.

JOY: You think I don't understand! *[She pick up her phone and dials]*

HOLLY: *[On the phone]* Hello darling. Yes. I'm at the house. Can you come home early? *[Addressed to James but directed at JOY]* I met this wonderful woman on the flight and I asked her to come and stay for a while.

JOY: *[On the phone]* Matthew? Better come here early tonight. Holly's been picking up strays again and she's brought this one home.

HOLLY: *[On the phone]* Well, I thought it might be nice to put on a good dinner for her, so you can all meet her.

Act I 5

JOY: *[On the phone]* Some cellist apparently. I'm not sure, Rachael something. Hang on. *[To HOLLY]* What's her other name?

HOLLY: *[On the phone]* Yes six. And bring a bottle of that New Zealand thing we had at that place – you know. *[To JOY]* I don't know. Maybe Martin?

JOY: You are incredible *[On the phone]* Did you hear that? Rachael Marlin? *[To HOLLY]* Is it Rachael Marlin?

HOLLY: *[On the phone]* No Joy's old room. *[To JOY]* That's it. *[On the phone]* She won't notice the golf clubs she dead to the world.

JOY: *[On the phone]* It is her. Who is she anyway? Auditioning for something apparently. I doubt it she'll probably fall asleep in her soup.

HOLLY: *[On the phone]* Don't worry. You can sneak in and get those when she comes down for dinner.

JOY: *[On the phone]* Come home with James.

HOLLY: *[On the phone]* Make sure you collect Matthew.

HOLLY: *[On the phone]* Bye.

JOY: *[On the phone]* Bye. *[To HOLLY]* Well this is getting interesting.

HOLLY: Why?

JOY: Mathew says that if it is Rachael Marlin, she's really big in Britain. She made some Bach recordings apparently, a few years ago, and everyone's nuts about them.

HOLLY: I knew she must be someone big. I can always pick them. Heavens! She must think I'm a bit of an idiot though. Fancy asking her to stay and not knowing who she is!

JOY: Well, you still don't really do you? Anyway, she was probably impressed that you had the temerity not to mention it. That's always my approach with famous people. I'm sure it makes them think I am really sophisticated and that I hang out with famous people all the time. Once I spent the whole night talking to Paul Kelly about music and didn't think to stop to ask him what he did.

HOLLY: I am sure he was really impressed.

JOY: Probably. But the truth is I didn't really know who he was anyway. He is a musician, isn't he? I thought he was a journalist or a football player or something?

HOLLY: Each of them is one of those.

JOY: What? I don't understand that at all. Anyway, none of this really gets us any closer to your reasons for bringing her home. Come on. Which of your pet projects is this one about? Are you trying to rope her into the Malvern Symphony?

Act I

HOLLY: It did cross my mind, although I suppose Matthew's news probably puts paid to that idea. No. I wasn't really thinking about that. Anyway, the Malvern Symph can look after itself. No, she just struck me as being really interesting. Quite normal really. Attractive but very simple. And the way she talked... she speaks very clearly... almost precisely and about some quite complicated ideas and emotions. The way she talked about music. She's really fascinating.

JOY: What did she say?

HOLLY: Oh, I don't remember exactly.

JOY: She can hardly be that fascinating then.

HOLLY: You know what I mean. It's not so much exactly what she says.

JOY: Form over content.

HOLLY: Exactly. But one thing I do remember is that she is very keen on, well you know, the music.

JOY: That hardly sounds like a revelation – for a musician.

HOLLY: No, I mean, she very focused. She gave me the impression that playing her instrument is the only really important thing to her and that everything else is, well, nothing. She never goes to concerts. She has no interest in the opera or the theatre or movies.

JOY: Sounds dull.

HOLLY: But she's not dull. She's utterly engaging and really quite impressive. *[Joy says nothing]* But for goodness sake, I haven't said anything about you and Matthew! *[Hugging her]* That was such good news.

JOY: I wondered whether you would be pleased.

HOLLY: Of course I'm pleased. What do you mean?

JOY: Well, you never really talk about him.

HOLLY: Nonsense. We talk about him all the time. You two are always first on our guest list – we love Matthew. All that music he does at the Grammar is terrific. I always knew you two would get married.

JOY: Well, perhaps that's it. Maybe I just thought you regarded Matthew as the sort of boy who comes up with the rations. You know, good first husband material.

HOLLY: That's not it at all. He's far from the ordinary. When I think of some of those characters you used to bring home!

JOY: See what I mean?

HOLLY: Stop it. You are being silly. Surely you don't think I am disapproving! Is that why you announced it when I was away?

Act I

JOY: It was hardly an 'announcement'. And I don't think you are disapproving. I guess I just thought that when it came to Matthew you were not really very impressed. Being impressed is a big thing with you.

HOLLY: Well, I am impressed and there is nothing wrong with marriage coming up with the rations. It gives order and regularity. Without order and regularity in your marriage, what on earth is the point of having affairs?

JOY: I'll bear that in mind.

HOLLY: Good God! Look at the time! I hope Maria remembered to put on the dinner. *[She moves into the kitchen and starts preparing dinner]* So when are you having the wedding?

JOY: Oh, I don't know. We thought we'd wait for a few months until we can get a booking at a venue.

HOLLY: *[Busy]* How many do you think you'll have?

JOY: No more than fifty.

HOLLY: Well, why don't you have a caterer and do it here whenever you like? We could ask Rachael to play.

JOY: Well, I think we had better meet her first. Anyway, I am not sure solo cello is quite the thing for the traditional bridal boogie.

We hear the front door open and the voices of MATTHEW and JAMES.

HOLLY: *[Preoccupied]* I suppose not. That sounds like James and Matthew. *[Calling]* Hello!

JAMES: *[Off]* The globetrotter is returned.

MATTHEW enters with JAMES behind him. JAMES goes to the kitchen where he kisses his wife as she makes dinner. MATTHEW kisses JOY in a self-consciously perfunctory manner.

JAMES: So where is Rachael Marlin?

HOLLY: She's upstairs sleeping.

JOY: So, you know all about her do you?

JAMES: I do, as a matter of fact.

JOY: What Bach cello suites are the big topic of conversation at drug company cocktail parties are they? I knew that 3MBS subscription I gave you last Christmas would come in handy.

JAMES: Not exactly, I haven't been able to find it on the tuner yet. The new Beamer auto-programmer doesn't seem to run to community radio.

JOY: Matt, give us the CD notes you just gave James on the way home and we'll all know all about her.

MATTHEW: I told you on the phone. She's done some solo work in the UK and her Bach recordings are really good, but she's not out there that much.

> She is a bit of a mystery actually. She doesn't really do any orchestral work. How did she strike you Holly?

HOLLY: That makes sense. She seems really very focused on just playing the cello – a real specialist, a virtuoso!

JAMES: I suppose she is really good looking? Have you noticed the way cellists are always really attractive - passionate!

JOY: Not compared to psychiatrists.

JAMES: Don't worry, my love, none of us physical paragons has anything on you gorgeous young doctors.

HOLLY: *[Approaching MATTHEW]* I don't think any of us has anything to worry about there. We're all extremely beautiful and devastatingly talented. I haven't kissed Matthew yet *[She does so]* who has been so talented as to decide to marry the best girl on the market *[She kisses JOY]* and, what is more, to get her to agree to it. Well done you.

MATTHEW: Even my students seem to be treating me with a modicum of respect since we got engaged. I am feeling pretty smug about it.

JOY: Well, you should be feeling nervous.

MATTHEW: Why nervous?

JOY: Because I'm trouble.

JAMES: Yes. Girls Grammar School Captain 2005 and Dean's List every year thereafter is a model of difficulty and irresponsibility.

JOY: But that's exactly it. All those years of conformity are bound to come bursting back at some point.

MATTHEW: Yeah, you'll probably find me on the morning after the wedding night completely mad and frothing at the mouth.

JAMES: We had better procure one of those tribal medicine men Freud talks about. Let him 'exercise the rites of the first night'! It is all in *The Taboo of Virginity*.

HOLLY: That 'first night' business always sounded vaguely theatrical to me.

MATTHEW: Except there are never any mad virgins on stage at any theatrical first night!

JOY: That's why they changed it to 'Opening Night'. You know, masses of previews beforehand.

HOLLY: *[Passing on a plate of nuts to MATTHEW]* This is all getting a bit too gynaecological for me. Here, put these nuts out. She'll probably be down in a minute.

JAMES: I think I'll get that French bottle we brought back last year so we can celebrate the marriage and our new star guest.

MATTHEW: *[Putting down the nuts]* I have to admit I am a bit excited to meet her. I have been listening to those recordings for years. I'd love to talk to her about them.

JOY: That's what you do in your study all night, is it?

MATTHEW: Would you rather I was down-loading porn?

JOY: Frankly I would be relieved.

HOLLY: Well, I am excited too. She is really delightful and it's a bonus that she is so impressive. I think it's going to be really fun having her about.

JAMES: *[Returning with a bottle]* Here it is. I thought Andrew and Francesca might have pinched it on our way back from Provance, but it was in the bar fridge. Shall I put it on ice? That thing doesn't really work. It just buzzes away all day keeping the coal industry afloat.

JOY: No. For God's sake open it right away.

As they talk RACHAEL enters, unselfconsciously, wearing only a summer robe and carrying a tea cup.

HOLLY: *[Racing over to her]* And here is the star attraction. Rachael, come in and meet everyone. This is James and our friend Joy and her fiancée Matthew.

General greetings.

RACHAEL: Hello everyone. I'm sorry I didn't want to disturb your evening. I just thought I'd pop down and get some tea.

HOLLY: Don't be silly, we're just about to have dinner. It's ready when you are.

JAMES: *[Approaching with the bottle]* And we've opened this especially for you.

RACHAEL: Oh, that's very kind of you, but I think I am going to have to just pop back into bed. I know that seems terribly rude, but I can't see myself keeping awake for more than about fifteen minutes. I hope you don't mind?

HOLLY: No, if you are sure. That's fine. Just pop back down if you can't sleep.

RACHAEL: Thanks. I will. And thanks for such a delightful welcome. Perhaps we can really have it at about four o'clock in the morning?

HOLLY: Of course! Of course!

RACHAEL: Goodnight everyone.

General good nighting. RACHAEL exits and all are a little dumbfounded.

JOY: Well, she is interesting.

HOLLY: Isn't she!

End Act.

ACT TWO

A few weeks have passed. In the lounge room as before, the couch backing onto the audience has been pushed aside and HOLLY, JAMES and MATTHEW are sitting on couches either side of RACHAEL who is in the middle of a recital playing Bach cello suites. It is a perfect performance and RACHAEL is totally immersed in her work. She should play a little too long so that the theatre audience start to get bored and wish for a lightly entertaining song, if only they would dare admit it. Eventually she finishes. The assembled family audience applauds.

HOLLY: That was just fantastic. Wasn't it? I haven't heard those Bach suites for so long and listening to them tonight reminded me of the first time I ever heard them. But the way you played them... I just can't say... Let's give her another round of applause, shall we? *[They all applaud again]* I have to say, I'm such a barbarian, but when I was listening to you rehearse this week Rachael, I was a little bit anxious about the length of the pieces – at least for our little soirée group.

JAMES: *[Interrupting]* Hey, speak for yourself.

HOLLY: I know, but we can't all be connoisseurs like you Jim. What I wanted to say was that I was wrong. Listening and really concentrating on these works tonight seemed to take me to a place where you just don't want it to end. Each note and each phrase seems completely fixed and in place and it's not until the end that you really feel this and start to see how it all works.

MATTHEW: That's right.

HOLLY: But beyond all the intellectualisation, the way I feel when I listen to Rachael play. I'm not sure exactly how she feels – she looks as if she feels it all so intensely – but I kind of think I'm there with her while she's playing. It's such a good feeling and such an honour. So, thank you, Rachael, you are such a star! *[She hands her some flowers and kisses her.]*

RACHAEL: Thank you, Holly. And thanks everyone for being here.

More applause.

HOLLY: Yes, thanks everyone. We're planning another evening next month. I hope Rachael will be free to play but she is very busy with auditions and other concert opportunities, so we'll have to wait and see. But I'll put it all in the next email and let you know. Do stay and finish the coffee, and the wine of course. James will you? And many thanks once again.

Polite applause. Soon a lighting change indicates a time jump. The audience are now gone and the family are left behind clearing up and finishing off the food and drink.

HOLLY: That went really well I think.

Act ii

RACHAEL: Good. I really enjoyed it.

JAMES: So did I. And I wasn't nodding off, thank you Joy. I was meditating. I am sick of spending all my life telling my clients to do it and not getting the benefit of it myself, so I decided to try it out with the help of Rachael and Johann Sebastian. You don't mind, do you Rachael?

RACHAEL: Whatever works, Jim.

MATTHEW: Well, I thought it went particularly well. I'll have to bring some of my students next time.

JOY: You played beautifully, Rachael. And don't take any notice of Holly's public rhetoric about it being too long. She seems to think it's her job to pander to a perceived bogan element in the audience when it doesn't really exist.

HOLLY: That's not true.

JOY: It's so condescending, Holly. Really. These people show up and listen and they thoroughly enjoy themselves. Just because they don't blab on about "each phrase being perfectly fixed in place" doesn't mean they don't engage. If they were bogans they could just as easily stay at home and watch *20 to One* or *The Footy Show*.

HOLLY: I know, but if I put out the rank bums on seats point of view it gives the impression that I understand anyone who does feel it's a bit highbrow.

JOY: Yes, but you don't have to. You don't have to apologise. Especially with this crowd. In the end it makes you look like a bogan.

HOLLY: Well, I was a bogan before you were even born, so I don't have any problem with that.

MATTHEW: So, Rachael, how are the auditions going?

RACHAEL: There have been a lot of them, but they have been going really well. I had a really good workshop with the MSO the other day, but no hard offers yet.

MATTHEW: That's frustrating.

RACHAEL: It is a bit. It's fairly tiring too, but I am enjoying myself.

JAMES: How long do you think you will have to wait?

RACHAEL: It could be a while. Nothing in that world moves very quickly.

JOY: You're not getting bored?

HOLLY: Well, I'm not. She's practising all day here. I love it! It's like having my own personal soloist in the house.

RACHAEL: No. I'm never really bored when I am hard at it.

JOY: Matthew, why don't you find her some teaching while she's waiting?

MATTHEW: I suppose I could.

RACHAEL: That's kind, but I wouldn't if I were you.

MATTHEW: Why not?

RACHAEL: I'm a terrible teacher. I just can't concentrate. If I get a really good student, or even a really bad one for that matter, I just focus in on what they are playing and start dreaming. I'm not any good at correcting and helping students improve. One student I had years ago couldn't manage to get off 'Old MacDonald' because she played it so well and I just kept getting her to do it again. Her parents were really mad.

JOY: That doesn't sound a bad thing – particularly for beginners.

RACHAEL: I gave it up years ago. More time for my practice, I suppose.

MATTHEW: What about some ensemble work?

RACHAEL: I am afraid I don't have a good track record with small groups either. I do sound a bit antisocial don't I?

JOY: She's an individual. We should leave her alone.

HOLLY: Precisely. What's more we should also let her get some sleep.

MATTHEW: Sorry, I wasn't trying to push you into anything.

RACHAEL: Of course not. That's fine. It's a perfectly normal suggestion. It's just that I am not exactly normal when it comes to these things. 'Perverse' is probably a better description of how I go about my business.

JAMES: Now that does sound interesting.

HOLLY: Well, you can save it for your consultation hour, Jim. Let's go to bed, I'm tired.

JAMES: No, I think I'll stay here and talk perversion with Rachel if you don't mind.

HOLLY: I don't mind. But I am sure Rachael has fairly defined views on the subject.

RACHAEL: To be honest I'm still wide awake.

JOY: So, five minutes with James should do the trick. Just don't let him put you under hypnosis, Rachael.

JAMES: *[As if exiting]* Pour us another drink, Rachael. I just need the loo.

RACHAEL: OK.

HOLLY: I suppose we had better clear some of this up otherwise tomorrow morning will be a nightmare.

JOY: We'll help.

MATTHEW: Yes, I am still a little drunk. Cleaning up after parties and breaking a few glasses is usually the best way to confirm that fact.

Act ii

JOY, HOLLY and MATTHEW clean up, each of them keeping half an eye on what is going on between RACHAEL and JAMES. Soon JAMES returns from the other side of the room – he has not quite been able to leave – and Rachael, who has not seen this, hands him a drink. As she does this JAMES clasps her hand romantically.

RACHAEL: What's this?

JAMES: I'm just trying to seduce you from a standing start.

RACHAEL: *[She laughs and takes back her hand]* Is that wise?

JAMES: I don't see why not. I am hardly any more effective with a warm-up.

RACHAEL: So you don't imagine that you will be successful.

JAMES: I don't know. I wouldn't think it was out of the realms of possibility.

RACHAEL: I think it might just be.

JAMES: Oh really? *[Sitting down]* Well, at least we can get on with our drink, and our conversation, without the fear of that coming up again.

RACHAEL: No. You don't get away with it that easily.

JAMES: That's a great pity.

RACHAEL: What do you mean?

JAMES: I was hoping we'd either be in bed by now, or that my embarrassing little declaration would have forced us to sublimate the sexual tension with a wide-ranging discourse on Debussy.

RACHAEL: This is hardly the moment for Debussy. Anyway, where does all this sexual tension come from?

JAMES: It's not all that sexual you know. Besides, I thought you'd think that, so I took care of that side of things in the bathroom just now.

RACHAEL: Darling, you think of everything.

JAMES: You're not offended?

RACHAEL: I'm certainly not excited, but I'm not offended either. I suppose I'm interested. I never really think of myself as attractive to anyone, so I'm always fascinated when someone shows some interest. As well as being a little bit sceptical. Why do you want to go to bed with me?

JAMES: I've been thinking about it for a while. Since you came to stay I've developed some quite significant feelings for you. I really look forward to seeing you every day. When you do the smallest thing for me, like hand me a glass of wine or repeat something I have said, I feel incredibly warmed by it. I suppose going to bed with you is simply the most appropriate response to the situation.

RACHAEL: So it's really not about the sex?

Act ii

JAMES: How could it be? We've never been to bed before, so I have no idea if it would be any good. From my dim recollections of pre-Holly encounters, and one or two very minor indiscretions since, all I can really remember is that going to bed with anyone for the first time usually turns out to be rubbish. Why on earth do you think one-night stands are so popular?

RACHAEL: And follow-up sex is comparatively rare!

JOY: *[To HOLLY]* Your plans for Rachael seem to be moving along nicely.

HOLLY: What do you mean by that?

JOY: Well, look at them.

RACHAEL: Did you really manage to get yourself off in the bathroom just now?

HOLLY: *[To JOY]* What?

JAMES: *[Laughing]* Of course not! I couldn't actually leave the room for some reason. But even if I had, the one thing I will say about my skill as a lover is that I am never that quick.

MATTHEW: *[Trying to close a cupboard door]* Holly, I don't actually seem to be able to get this in.

RACHAEL: So, are you in love with me?

JAMES: Of course!

RACHAEL: Really? I had no idea!

JAMES: I didn't think you did.

RACHAEL: Does that mean that you are disenchanted with your marriage?

JAMES: No. I am pretty sure that if we acted on it in a sustained fashion it would lead to an atmosphere of disenchantment – at least from a practical standpoint. But from your response, I assume that's not going to happen.

RACHAEL: No.

JAMES: Fine.

RACHAEL: I haven't broken your heart?

JAMES: Now you really want some honey! Well, I'm not really going to give you too much. You may have broken my heart. As I say I've been thinking about this a lot over the last few weeks, but I also know that this is one of the outcomes of falling in love. But I don't feel heartbroken now. In fact I feel happy.

RACHAEL: Why? Are you relieved?

JAMES: A little. But I've had the thrill of telling you how I feel about you. In fact I could easily go on all night. Don't misunderstand me. Now that I've relieved myself verbally I am starting to think that there is nothing I'd rather do than go to bed with you.

RACHAEL: It's such a disturbing thing when love turns to sexual desire.

JAMES:	Exactly. We should have gone to bed weeks ago and the whole thing would have been nipped in the bud immediately.
JOY:	Holly, you have got to go in there and break them up. Poor Jim looks petrified. He actually looks like he might just be about to score.
HOLLY:	Don't be ridiculous.
MATTHEW:	I am perfectly prepared to go in there and take one for the team.

JAMES and RACHAEL are becoming increasingly aware of the others' conversation.

JAMES:	I may not have offended you, but I have startled you a bit, I think?
RACHAEL:	No. I have just run out of things to say.
JAMES:	So, you are not upset or annoyed? You are not going to pack your bags and head out the door?
RACHAEL:	No. Unless you want me to?
JAMES:	Of course not. But do you have any response to what I've said?
JOY:	OK, this is getting interesting and I am getting quite nostalgic.
HOLLY:	Joy!

JOY approaches JAMES and RACHAEL.

RACHAEL: *[Formally, in just above a whisper]* I don't wish to seem ungrateful. You have all been so kind to me. But I must decline your offer while thanking you for it. I never saw it coming, which is why I feel I am in no position to accept it, or act upon it in any way. Please do not think me rude if I ask you, earnestly, not to make your offer again, but to still keep me in your thoughts and prayers as a kind and affectionate friend.

JOY sits.

JOY: I'm still wide awake too. But actually, James, when did I need an excuse to hang about late after the audience have gone? I really love this part best of all. Whatever the show is, 'whenever two or more are gathered together' afterwards there is always this delightful emotional residue. It's a kind of a faint, fading impression of everything that happened over the last couple of hours. It's like you can feel the stardust settling. I can't get enough of it.

End Act.

ACT THREE

A few weeks have passed. The lounge room is set as it was in Act Two. RACHAEL is playing a composition of her own. It is of such exquisite beauty and technical virtuosity that it cannot fail to bore the audience to death. As always, RACHAEL is clearly transported by the work and plays it to the peak of her ability and with the highest levels of concentration and immersion. When the piece comes to its conclusion it is not at all obvious to the audience. Nor does RACHAEL look up or give any indication that it is over or beg for applause to relieve the tension. She is not self-conscious about the audience's reaction to the work. She is very simply satisfied. When the tension has become unbearable, HOLLY, not sure herself if the piece is over, jumps up to speak.

HOLLY: Do you know, as always, I prepared a silly little speech about how marvellous this work is, and how fantastic Rachael is, but I'm not going to give it! What can I say? I am 'bewitched, bothered and bewildered' but above all – totally speechless.

Before the applause can interrupt, the lights go to black and there is a repeat of the scene change experienced at the beginning of the last act. When the lights come back on RACHAEL and MATTHEW are seated as JOY, HOLLY and JAMES are packing up.

JAMES: Before she played that I was really not in the mood to listen to it.

JOY: And now you're still not?

JAMES: Got it in one, my love. Each phrase seemed perfectly fixed in place to penetrate the inner recesses of my rectum.

HOLLY: She's finally located your inner bogan, has she Jim?

MATTHEW: I think you upset the applecart tonight.

RACHAEL: What do you mean? Did I bore them?

MATTHEW: No, it's not that. They are used to a carefully selected program of Baroque favourites. This stuff is too modern, too difficult, too...

RACHAEL: Don't say it!

MATTHEW: Don't say what?

RACHAEL: "They don't understand me."

MATTHEW: *[Laughing]* That is not true. Or at least it's not any truer than it was last month when you played Bach.

RACHAEL: But they liked me then.

MATTHEW: There's something disappointing in that admission. And something vaguely attractive too.

Act iii

JOY: *[To HOLLY and JAMES]* Well, I think it's Holly's fault. She's pampering her.

RACHAEL: *[To MATTHEW]* Meaning?

MATTHEW: Since when did you care whether people liked you or not?

RACHAEL: So, what is attractive about disappointing people's expectations?

MATTHEW: Don't you know? It is one of the great sources of attraction. We only really begin to admire an artist, or a person for that matter, when we see them going through a grey period.

RACHAEL: Now that you think I have feet of clay like everyone else, you suddenly think I am attractive? Well, it may work for you, but it seems to have exactly the opposite effect on everyone else. Note the empty dressing room, the embarrassingly denuded state of the vases and, above all, the thronging absence of fans and well-wishers!

MATTHEW: But that is just it! I am the only one that can see it. If anyone else thought you had stuffed up tonight you would be batting them away with your bow. There was nothing wrong with tonight. In fact, to compare it with last time, it was probably slightly better. Any performance that manages to shut Holly up has to be considered seriously. In fact, that is exactly why everyone left so early. What do you want from this audience? People yapping platitudes or mounting impertinent little interpretations of your work? Jesus, girl! Play your piece, take your bow, go home to bed and thank God you don't have to endure the appalling notoriety of apparently well-meaning criticism.

JOY: What is she here for, Holly?

RACHAEL: Sometimes we all have a little crisis of confidence.

MATTHEW: Of course we do, but not you. You have no right to a crisis of confidence at all. Especially not tonight.

RACHAEL: Why not?

MATTHEW: Because you have probably just given the performance of your lifetime.

RACHAEL: What here?

MATTHEW: O ye of little faith! I know, it's ironic isn't it. We all dream of the perfect show when everything comes together, we are playing at our best and most engaged, the audience are dazzled but seem to be copying down each note in their minds, the bliss is unconfined and leaves everyone mute. It is the prefect dream of a great concert-hall performance and we end up really doing it for Holly and her occasional Friday night Salon. Or, what is worse, we do it in rehearsal.

RACHAEL: So, was that it?

MATTHEW: Probably. Or when it is 'it' it will probably be something just like it. Don't you remember the sceptical priest in *La Dolce Vita*? Miracles

Act iii

happen in peace and quiet, not in mass chaos and confusion. It is a bit like having great sex. It's not usually an achievement you can expect any applause for – apart from a possible audience of one, or a few more depending on your particular perversion.

RACHAEL: But at a certain point you really have to deal with your audience.

MATTHEW: What makes you think you don't?

RACHAEL: I don't think about them enough. Or at least I get the feeling from people that I don't. Holly and her little comments about highbrow art, you and your teaching patronage. I am no good at the 'outreach' stuff. I don't enjoy it.

MATTHEW: But it is not about mass engagement – dealing with the audience. It is about the way you define your audience – who you can expect to speak to. If you want to engage me on that level I am sure I'll provide sufficient appreciation.

JOY: *[To HOLLY]* Is she here for the same reason I was?

RACHAEL: You are back to perversions again, aren't you?

MATTHEW: I never left them.

HOLLY: *[To JAMES]* Why did we have Joy here, James?

JAMES: *[Distracted]* God! Her parents were hopeless.

RACHAEL: *[Throws pillow at him]* Idiot.

JAMES: What are we doing, children? Pillow fights at our age? I'll have to put you both over my knee and spank your little bottoms.

RACHAEL: *[Getting up to leave with a smile]* You would probably enjoy it more if you just thought about it after. A fuse blows and the lights go out leaving them in the dark.

RACHAEL leaves unnoticed. The following scene is played in complete darkness.

JOY: What was that?

JAMES: It was probably that bloody fuse box again. I'll try to find the torch and Matthew you see if you can get the cellar door up.

JOY: So, all James' idea was it Holly? Nothing to do with you?

HOLLY: Don't tell me it's still down there? You said you were going to get the electrician to move it when he updated the wiring.

JAMES: Yes. Well, when he updates the wiring we can get him to move the fuse box.

MATTHEW is feeling around the kitchen floor for the cellar door while JAMES is off looking for a torch. Soon JAMES returns but with only a box of matches. MATTHEW flicks it on as they talk, but it keeps going out.

JAMES: Here try this. I couldn't find the torch.

Act iii

JOY: Funny. I always wondered if it was your idea.

HOLLY: Or the candles apparently! At least in a crisis James can always manage to find a box of matches!

MATTHEW: Wonderful infrastructure here. Here it is I think. *[He pulls up the cellar door.]* God. What is that smell?

JAMES: It's not a wine smell is it?

MATTHEW: No. It's more like an Apple Mac has come down her to die alone. Hang on, is that smoke?

JAMES: Surely not. The fuse box wouldn't smoke would it?

JOY: I was here for the same reason Rachael's here?

HOLLY: Unlike some people.

JAMES: Do shut up, Holly.

HOLLY: Just trying to lighten the mood a bit.

MATTHEW: I don't think so. I'll just get in and have a look.

JAMES: Hang on Matthew. Are you sure you want to go in there? It's dark and it does smell pretty bad.

MATTHEW: It should be fine. I've been in there before.

JAMES: But, as you say, I haven't had that thing looked at for years. I wouldn't want you to stumble over something you can't handle. It could be dangerous.

MATTHEW: No, it's fine.

JAMES: I really wouldn't you know. You might do yourself a great deal of harm.

MATTHEW: You are probably right. It does really smell like death down there.

> *JAMES: We can have a look at it in the morning. Pause. After a moment the lights come back on. RACHAEL has gone but nobody mentions it. JAMES returns to the kitchen to look for things in the drawer and HOLLY momentarily fusses there too. MATTHEW is sitting wondering what just happened and JOY joins him in an attempt to find out.*

JOY: Matthew, what is going to happen with Rachael?

> *MATTHEW pauses a minute, considering which implied question to answer.*

MATTHEW: As far as I know she's going to keep auditioning and hope something comes of it.

JOY: She doesn't have any money worries or anything?

MATTHEW: I doubt it.

JOY: *[To HOLLY]* You're not charging her rent I hope?

HOLLY: I'm not actually, but she insists on giving me a more than reasonable amount every month.

JAMES: It's not that reasonable.

HOLLY: Actually, it's more than reasonable given the size of her room and the fact she pays for her own food.

JOY: Well, I am worried about her.

MATTHEW: Really? Why?

JOY: I wonder if we are making it too easy for her? She's come here with this fantastic reputation and yet she can't get a real job. Her social and her, what should I say, her audience needs seem to be pretty low. We think we are helping her and yet perhaps we are just cocooning her in her own narcissism? Nice house. Nice friends. Nice little regular audience to satisfy her musically.

MATTHEW: It's not as if we are keeping her against her own will.

HOLLY: *[Growing frustrated]* Exactly.

JOY: Well, I'm not implying it's a question of enslavement.

HOLLY: And why should she have, what you call, 'a real job' anyway?

JAMES: That's ridiculous. Of course she wants a real job.

HOLLY: Why have you suddenly changed your attitude? You were besotted with her a few weeks ago.

JAMES: Because we've been having a vicious little affair and now I have to get rid of her.

HOLLY: Shut up James. No one finds your Byronic pervert persona funny anymore. Particularly as it's so improbable.

JAMES: It's the irony I'm going for. I had to give up the perversion when I married you.

MATTHEW: *[To JOY]* So, you think we're holding her back?

JOY: It's possible.

MATTHEW: And it's our duty to art to release her to find her own way?

JOY: You don't have to be as pompous as all that. A little bit superior will be perfectly adequate.

JAMES: Well, perhaps it is our duty to push her out of the nest. As pompous as that may sound.

HOLLY: For God's sake listen to yourselves. Could this conversation get any more ridiculous? The woman is paying her bills, she's not harming anyone and all she wants to do is to get on with her work in her own way. And yet, for some reason, this is presenting you lot with some apparent crisis of obligation. You don't care about Rachael, you don't care about her work and you certainly don't give a damn about art. Let's face it. We are beyond art. We are so bloody drowning in it, fucking film festivals every week of the year, winter blockbusters at the gallery and opera on Sydney Harbour, as well as all over the bloody web and on pirate downloads. We just expect it to be poured over us like brandy on the Christmas pudding. And yet when we come across someone actually doing it, in a simple and unassuming way, and not giving a toss what we think about it, we can't cope and we reject it. This isn't about art, it's about commerce and big is beautiful. She's got a perfectly good product and we are so beyond the simplicity of it that we can't stand the fact that she doesn't want to expand it – put it on ice or suspend it from a bridge on the Yarra. God, I actually heard some idiot the other night say to Rachael "that was a wonderful piece, dear, what are you going to do with it?" Jesus, she just did something with it, she played it. Can you understand how insulting that must be to her? She wrote it, she rehearsed it and she served it up to us for virtually nothing and then she gets told to 'do' something with it. Are people really so churlish or self-loathing that they think that being at a performance like that is only worthwhile if thousands of other people are willing to pay for it too?

JOY: That's not what they mean.

HOLLY: I know. They mean to be kind. Perhaps what they really mean is that this is all so fantastic that it should make you amount to something more. But isn't that the same thing? And how would you like it? "Nice medical practice you have been running for ten years, dear Dr Joy, what are you going to do with that?"

JOY: I don't think I'd mind very much.

HOLLY: No. You would probably just up your fee schedule. That would be doing something.

JAMES: I don't think I've ever heard you be nasty before.

HOLLY: Oh? I have an incredible ability to be nasty. Utilitarian too. Didn't you know, Jim? After all these years, it must have escaped you. I patronise people. I bring them into our house. I feed them. I encourage them. I find all sorts of ways to help them. Then suddenly, without even knowing it, I manage to seduce them into acting out my most extreme sexual and social fantasies. Vicariously, you know. I don't have to do a thing. At some point between knocking up a spanakopita and setting the dates for the soirées they suddenly start sleeping with you and trying it on with Matthew too. It's so easy for me. I don't have to lift a finger and, what is more, I get to watch.

JAMES: Holly, really!

HOLLY: That's what you are saying, isn't it Joy? It's nothing to do with art, is it? We're beyond art. Nature is above and beyond art in this, isn't it?

JOY: Of course it is.

End Act.

ACT FOUR

It is the next morning. The family are preparing Sunday lunch. Eventually RACHAEL enters and starts helping JOY, who is setting the table for four.

RACHAEL: You guys were up pretty late last night.

JOY: Yes, the evening did drag on a bit. You thought you were the show!

RACHAEL: You mean I was the warm-up act?

JOY: Oh yes. Matthew and James were the main event and the evening was rounded off with a sort of lecture by Holly.

RACHAEL: What was it about?

JOY: Patronage! That's what we do here. In fact, that is why we are all here.

RACHAEL: Including me?

JOY: Of course.

RACHAEL: Am I doing my bit? Fulfilling my role?

JOY: Probably depends on what you do now. How you react.

RACHAEL: How did you react when you found out?

JOY: Oh, I behaved beautifully. I was very subtle. You see I didn't come here on a music scholarship like you. I came here as a sort of white slave for James, and Holly was my protector. At first it was hard to see what would induce me to stay. But I worked it out eventually.

RACHAEL: What was it?

JOY: I suppose, I would say, the arousal of certain needs in me in the face of the charming expectations of others.

RACHAEL: How old were you? Eighteen? Nineteen? Can young women of that age really understand those kinds of needs, and that type of expectation?

JOY: You'd be surprised. In fact I think I understood it very well. Much more than poor old James.

RACHAEL: Poor old James?

JOY: Yes. Why do you say it like that?

RACHAEL: He's hardly the victim!

JOY: No. But it wasn't exactly his idea. And it didn't really amount to very much.

RACHAEL: Whose was it?

JOY: Holly's of course. James was really just a functionary in all that. I don't think he enjoyed himself at all. Even if he did, he's hardly the type to be really relaxed at the idea of being emotionally pimped to his god-daughter by his own wife.

RACHAEL: He's obviously pretty weak.

JOY: Of course.

RACHAEL: What about you?

JOY: I don't know. I suppose I must have been pretty weak too. I came here because I needed a family and my family were hopeless. I suppose if I had been less naïve I would have told them all to get stuffed. But I had a lot to learn.

RACHAEL: And did you learn much?

JOY: Not really. Wisdom came later, and so did practicality. You're not very practical, are you Rachael?

RACHAEL: Not really. At least not practical enough to put up with you lot any longer.

JOY: I understand. You see I am very practical. My marriage to Matthew is going to be very practical. And I think it is my turn to put out some of those charming expectations. I think Matthew understands that, God help him!

RACHAEL: Yes. I can see that.

JOY: I thought you would. *[Pause]* Do you think God, or the universe, really give a stuff about my marriage? Or your music for that matter?

RACHAEL: No. Not at all.

JOY: You're probably right. But I do care, you see. My practicality and your lack of it are very important to me.

RACHAEL: I can see that too.

HOLLY: What are you two talking about?

JOY: Rachael is sounding me out about how we would all cope if she abandoned us. It seems she is getting far too settled in our domestic regime.

RACHAEL: That's right. You see I need doubt and uncertainty to thrive. I am getting far too comfortable to be of any use to you or to myself.

HOLLY: That's nonsense. I don't buy that struggling artist myth for anything. Frankly Rachael, I'm surprised to hear you are succumbing to it.

RACHAEL: I don't know. It's still pretty potent. There is a fair bit of mileage in it yet.

HOLLY: Maybe. But it's no good to you, so far as I can see. We are the ones that need the suffering artist, not you lot. But personally, if I thought you were going to compose or play any better without a bed to sleep in, I would have turned you out of the house in a minute.

JOY: Noble sacrifice, hey Holly?

Act IV

HOLLY: Not at all. In fact, I am not interested in art that comes out of struggle in the slightest. Leave that to the media and the philanthropists. No, I am far more interested in the sort of work that comes out of privilege, inheritance, endowment and security. Any idiot can create out of struggle. But to make something out of the incredible disadvantage of entitlement – now that is brilliant.

RACHAEL: My dirty secret is out. I am obviously a talentless hack. A few months of good linen and central heating and my mediocrity has been exposed.

JOY: Never mind. I am sure you will be easily able to hide it playing at weddings and cocktail parties. In fact, do you know Rachael, before I even met you Holly was trying to line you up to play at my wedding.

RACHAEL: So, you never really had any faith in me in the first place?

HOLLY: I did actually. I just thought I would keep the wedding idea in my pocket to threaten you with if you became too lacking in complacency.

RACHAEL: Well, if you are threatening me with it now, I will have to decline or else I will disappoint you.

HOLLY: Good girl, now I can let you go. Fly the nest, thrive and prosper! *[Kisses her]*

JAMES: Watching women kiss is the foundation of one of my most significant sexual fantasies.

MATTHEW: Me too, actually. Why is that, do you think?

JAMES: Well, I'm still working on my theory, but I am convinced it has something to do with single-sex eduction.

MATTHEW: It is certainly very reassuring to watch.

JOY: They are not making out, they are making up.

HOLLY: Yes. Rachael was asking for my permission to run off with James and I took it the wrong way.

JAMES: That is very touching.

HOLLY: Not really. I just failed to see the positive side of the affair.

JOY: So I offered up you, Matthew, instead, but Rachael wasn't interested.

RACHAEL: Perhaps, on that note, it might be time for me to leave?

MATTHEW: Well, if you have refused Joy's offer, I can't really see any reason for you to stay.

RACHAEL: *[Looking at the table]* I'll go and pack my things.

JAMES: No. Why don't you leave that until after lunch?

MATTHEW: Yes. We can't send you off in disgrace with an empty stomach.

RACHAEL: I'll survive. *[She leaves the room]*

JAMES: *[Looking at the table]* I can really be such a complete bastard at times.

Act IV

JOY: Why do you say that?

JAMES: No, I really can be.

JOY: I am not denying it. I just want to know why you are reminding yourself at this particular moment.

HOLLY: *[Seeing him looking at the table.]* Look at the table. It's set for four.

JAMES: God, I'm an idiot. I was thinking she was looking at the table because she was hungry.

MATTHEW: Well, quick, set another place so when she comes back in she will appreciate the gesture and we can convince her to stay.

JAMES: She'll stay for lunch then at least. *[Nothing happens; JAMES looks at JOY then HOLLY]* Oh, right. Come on Matthew. Help me!

JAMES rushes into the kitchen to get an extra place setting. MATTHEW cottons on and finally starts to make space on the table. JOY and HOLLY look on with mild amusement. Before the fifth place is set, RACHAEL returns.

JAMES: Rachael, please stay for lunch.

RACHAEL: I'm not really going at all. I was about to but then I stopped myself. I realised exactly how this is all going to end. In fact, it doesn't have to end at all. We just have to put everything right.

MATTHEW: What do you mean?

RACHAEL: *[Walking to her cello case and getting it out]* Now Matthew and James. I want you to stop setting that extra place. Joy and I set the table, we knew perfectly well what we were doing. I want you all to sit down and eat your meal and I'll sit over here and play.

JAMES: Hang on. I think you have pretty well sung for your supper here, Rachael. Please just join us.

RACHAEL: It's really not necessary. You sit, relax, eat and I'll do the same over here and play.

HOLLY: Can we make requests?

RACHAEL: Of course, you can. But you have to pay. Say five dollars a request?

JOY: Ten dollars! Make it ten!

RACHAEL: OK. Ten dollars for a request.

HOLLY: But anything else you play you do for free.

JOY: Exactly. And if you play anything of your own, you have to pay us five dollars.

HOLLY: That's not fair.

JOY: No, you are right. She has to give us credit.

RACHAEL: Deal.

HOLLY: I suppose that is fair.

Act IV

JAMES: Hang on. This is all a bit awkward isn't it?

HOLLY: What do you mean?

MATTHEW: Yeah. We sit up here like the gentry and she's over there like the hired help.

JAMES: Yes. He's right. I don't like it.

HOLLY: Oh, come on you two. You'll get used to it.

JAMES: But I am not really comfortable with it.

RACHAEL: I don't see why. You have been doing it all along. It's not that you are uncomfortable with it, James. You are uncomfortable thinking about it. I'm the one who has been really uncomfortable. When I first came here I thought you were going to do the right thing and put me to work. But then you started easing me out of it, putting me on light duties and killing me with kindness. Do you think I am at ease sitting down to dinner with you guys, being made welcome at family functions, having my triumphs celebrated at impromptu cocktail parties? I can't stand it. It's such a relief when someone asks me to play. You see, I have an utter aversion to the simple pleasures of the punter. I am sick. Haven't you noticed when Holly has other musos playing? I have to sit on the aisle or slip in at the back. Hell, when Vika and Linda played the whole gig the other night I got so desperate I had to slip out the back and help the bar staff stock the fridge.

JAMES: So what you are saying is that you are a sort of musical masochist?

RACHAEL: That is right, utterly servile. I am really a musical, recreational hooker. I have to play before any audience I can scrape together and it really only turns me on when I get paid for it. So, if you really want to make me feel at home, sit down, eat, make as much noise as you like, pretend to listen every now and then, even clap sometimes, and I'll be as happy as Larry. Can I start off with a request?

JOY: Yes Bach. But hang on, credit's no good here. *[Grabbing her purse]* Come on everyone, cash down now.

As all reach for their cash, JOY rushes over. She opens Rachael's cello case on the ground and tosses in a ten-dollar note, then returns to the table. RACHAEL starts playing Bach. After a short passage HOLLY approaches RACHAEL and drops in some gold coins.

HOLLY: Can I get one Ravel and one of your own compositions? So that's five dollars.

RACHAEL nods and keeps playing. Matthew simply approaches and drops a few coins in the case in the rather self-conscious and condescending way common to the beneficiaries of buskers. RACHAEL replies with the typically zealous nod of gratitude common to buskers. After a while...

HOLLY: You know, this is really rather good.

Act IV

JOY: I don't feel uncomfortable at all. What do you think Matthew?

MATTHEW: I think I could get used to it. Rachael is obviously feeling more comfortable.

HOLLY: What do you think, James?

JAMES: Well, you know what I think about buskers in restaurants and on trains. I really resent being forced to listen to them and then feeling obliged to give then a few coins. But when it's in your own home I suppose I can see a place for it.

JOY: Good, then lend me ten dollars. If I don't drop it in the case before the Ravel ends she may revert to something of her own.

HOLLY: I wouldn't worry about that. By the looks of her, I doubt she can afford it.

RACHAEL plays out as the rest of them finish lunch and the lights fade.

Curtain.

www.ingramcontent.com/pod-product-compliance
Lightning Source LLC
Chambersburg PA
CBHW071320080526
44587CB00018B/3301